How to Respond to . . .

THE JEHOVAH'S WITNESSES

Herbert Kern

Publishing House
St. Louis

THE RESPONSE SERIES

How to Respond to the Cults
How to Respond to Transcendental Meditation
How to Respond to the Lodge
How to Respond to the Latter-day Saints
How to Respond to the Occult
How to Respond to Jehovah's Witnesses
How to Respond to the Eastern Religions
How to Respond to New Christian Religions
How to Respond to Islam
How to Respond to the Science Religions
How to Respond to Satanism
How to Respond to the New Age Movement
How to Respond to Secular Humanism
How to Respond to Judaism

Copyright © 1977, 1991 Concordia Publishing House
3558 S. Jefferson Avenue, St. Louis, MO 63118-3968
Manufactured in the United States of America

Library of Congress Cataloging in Publication Data

Kern, Herbert, 1917–
     How to respond to . . . the Jehovah's Witness.

     (Response series)
     Bibliography: p.
     1. Jehovah's Witnesses—Doctrinal and controversial works.
I. Title.
BX8526.K47   230'.9'9   77-23742
ISBN 0-570-07679-X

20   21   22   23   24   25   26   98   97   96   95   94   93   92   91

Foreword to the Response Series

Most of us have either received one of several publications from the Jehovah's Witnesses' Watch Tower Society, or received a friendly and persuasive team of Jehovah's Witnesses at our door with their own Bible version and theological arguments that label our beliefs as Satanic. They take their name—Witnesses—seriously. It takes an average of 740 house calls to recruit each of the nearly 200,000 people who yearly join their cult.

Because of such groups, The Lutheran Church—Missouri Synod in its 1975 Convention requested specialized literature to assist in the defense of our faith and in the evangelization of persons who belong to cults, sects, and other non-Christian religious movements. This series of booklets responds to that need as it compares the basic teachings of cults and other religious groups with the teachings of the Christian faith. St. Peter sums up the spirit of these booklets: "Always be prepared to give an answer to everyone who asks you to give the reason for the hope that you have. But do this with gentleness and respect" (1 Peter 3:15 NIV).

This second edition includes essential updates and will help you know more about the Jehovah's Witnesses—their refusal to accept blood transfusions or salute the flag, and their denial of Jesus' deity, the Trinity, and the existence of hell. Armed with this booklet, you will be better able to witness to Jehovah's Witnesses, and help those who are confused or affected by its teachings. You can then witness by the power of the Holy Spirit, from the Holy Scriptures, sharing the Good News that members of this cult so desperately need to hear: Jehovah is Jesus, the Lord, true man and also true God.

We pray that this booklet will be a valuable resource for you, both in your personal reading and in group study, so we may all be faithful witnesses of our risen Lord!

> Lyle D. Muller, *Executive Director*
> Board for Evangelism Services
> The Lutheran Church—Missouri Synod

Editor's Preface

Pastor Herbert Kern has taken a special interest in witnessing to Jehovah's Witnesses ever since he arranged a debate with Jehovah's Witnesses at his church in early 1957. He has gathered a library of Jehovah's Witnesses' publications and is thoroughly acquainted with their doctrines. *"Exactly* what does the Bible say?" is the question with which Pastor Kern approaches his subject matter, recognizing that distortions of the Bible's words can give rise to serious doctrinal errors.

Pastor Kern, after graduation from Concordia Seminary, St. Louis, in 1941, served in various missionary activities, including tent evangelism for five summers, religious census taking, planning new churches, and speaking at many churches. He has also served as an instructor at Concordia College, Bronxville, N.Y. For 31 years, he was a member of the research committee for the International Lutheran Hour radio broadcast. He served as pastor of Calvary Lutheran Church, East Meadow, Long Island, N.Y. for 32 years until his retirement in 1982. Since then he has lectured widely on witnessing to Jehovah's Witnesses and has been actively engaged in evangelism in the church at large and with his home congregation.

Eldon K. Winker, *Executive Secretary*
The Commission on Organizations
The Lutheran Church—Missouri Synod

Note

This booklet has been written with a prayerful concern for Jehovah's Witnesses and those exposed to their anti-Biblical teachings.

A short work of this kind can deal only with the central teachings of Scripture.

I am deeply indebted to the late Mrs. Bruce Jackson for her invaluable assistance. Mrs. Jackson, a pastor's wife, had thoroughly studied the Jehovah's Witnesses' doctrines and had been used by the Lord to lead a number of Jehovah's Witnesses out of darkness into the light of truth.

As you read this booklet, ask the Lord to open your mind to understand the Scriptures (Luke 24:45). I recommend that individual chapters be used for private and group study.

Herbert Kern

Contents

1

Historical Background of Jehovah's Witnesses

Charles Taze Russell founded the organization known since 1931 as the Jehovah's Witnesses. The first president of the Witnesses, he authored six of the seven volumes entitled *Studies in the Scriptures.* During the early history of the organization, these books formed the cornerstone of Jehovah's Witnesses' beliefs. In 1879 Russell first published *Zion's Watch Tower and Herald of Christ's Presence,* the forerunner of the organization's leading magazine, *The Watchtower.* Zion's Watch Tower Tract Society—now called Watch Tower Bible and Tract Society—was formed in 1881. It is the legal corporation for Jehovah's Witnesses. Russell boldly denied the deity of Jesus Christ. This fundamental error led to the rejection of other basic beliefs of Christianity.

The history of the Jehovah's Witnesses is inextricably bound to the teachings of Russell and the presidents who followed him—Joseph F. Rutherford (1917–42), Nathan H. Knorr (1942–77), and Frederick W. Franz (1977 to the present). All three men are noted for their many doctrinal writings and their organizational ability.

The January 1, 1991 issue of *The Watchtower* reported that there were 4,553,721 active Witnesses in 63,016 congregations in 212 countries in 1990. This was a 6.1% increase over the previous year. Local congregations meet in Kingdom Halls. Approximately 21% of the members of the organization live in the United States. The total number of people who attended the annual Memorial (Holy Communion service) in 1990 was 9,950,058. Of these only 8,869 (who consider themselves part of the elite 144,000) partook of the "emblems" of bread and wine. Jehovah's Witnesses recognize that those who claim to be Christians but show little faith are prime candidates for their persistent witnessing.

The Watchtower Society often mentions the adversity that the organization's beliefs and actions produce. This opposition stems, in part, from the Witnesses' constant denunciation of Christendom as the "devil's organization" and of all other organized religions. Other causes of antagonism are their refusal to salute the flag or bear arms for any country, their firm opposition to blood transfusions, and the manner in which they have spread their doctrines resulting in considerable legal problems and lawsuits under the First Amendment. Another characteristic of the cult is that it promises "knowledge" to its members. Jehovah's Witnesses are willing to devote much time teaching the unsuspecting—always, of course, with Watchtower helps. This has a strong appeal for people who are dissatisfied with their church and want to learn more about the Bible.

The Watchtower Society's translation of the Bible, the New World Translation, contains many significant errors, particularly in connection with the deity of Jesus Christ. The Brooklyn, N.Y. headquarters produces an enormous flood of doctrinal booklets and pamphlets written by anonymous authors. The major magazine in addition to *The Watchtower* is *Awake!* The former is published twice per month in 111 languages with an average printing of each issue in January, 1991 of 15,290,000.

All Watchtower materials are held to contain no error of doctrine at the time of their writing. Prophecies and interpretations stated today, however, may be altered in the future, as has happened time and again in the past. For example, until 1929 "the governing authorities" referred to in Rom. 13:1 were said to be "the earthly rulers." From 1929 to 1962 it was Jehovah's Witnesses' teaching that "the governing authorities" were "the Most High God Jehovah and his exalted Son Jesus Christ." Since 1962 "the superior authorities" (New World Translation, revised 1984) are again "the political authorities of this world."

Jehovah's Witnesses claim that the Bible is their one and only source of inspiration. Yet they rely exclusively in their studying and witnessing on the doctrinal interpretations set forth in their Watchtower publications. The Watchtower organization is therefore not a zealous, fundamentalist sect. It is rather a non-Christian cult whose beliefs are shaped by a handful of men. These leaders, known as the governing body, insist that they are God's only channel of communication on earth today and that there is no salvation outside the Watchtower Society.

2

Jesus Christ—True Man and True God

According to Jehovah's Witnesses Jesus Christ has existed in three different, separate states:

1. Michael the archangel—in heaven before He appeared on earth.
   (You May Survive Armageddon into God's New World, 1955, p. 112)
2. A man—*only* a man while on earth
   (Is This Life All There Is?, 1974, p. 128)
3. Michael the archangel—in heaven now
   (You May Survive Armageddon into God's New World, 1965, p. 112)

What is the truth?

. . . Christ Jesus, who, though he was in the *form of God,* did not count equality with God a thing to be grasped, but emptied himself, taking the form of a servant, being born in the likeness of men. And being found in *human form* he humbled himself and became obedient unto death, even death on a cross (Phil. 2:5-8).

Father, glorify Thou me in Thy own presence with the glory which I had with Thee before the world was made (John 17:5).

In Him all the fulness of God was pleased to dwell (Col. 1:19).

In Him the whole fulness of Deity dwells bodily (Col. 2:9).

Before the world began or any creature existed, Jesus Christ had the form or nature of God and possessed the same divine glory as His Father. He is equal with the Father (John 5:18) from eternity.

Jesus did not think His equality with God was to be eagerly clung to or retained. When He took the form or nature of a human being, He emptied Himself, that is, He did not always make full use of His divine power, knowledge, and other qualities. Yet His divine nature never changed. He has always been God.

As true man	As true God
He—was born in Bethlehem (Matt. 2:1).	He—said, Before Abraham was, I am (John 8:58).
was the son of man (Luke 19:10).	was the Son of God (John 20:31).
was hungry (Luke 4:2).	fed the multitudes (John 6:5 etc.).
	said, I am the bread of life (John 6:35).
said, I thirst (John 19:28).	said, If any one thirst, let him come to me and drink (John 7:37).
was weary (John 4:6).	said, Come to me, all who labor and are heavy laden, and I will give you rest (Matt. 11:28).
was troubled in spirit (John 13:21).	said, Let not your hearts be troubled (John 14:1).
prayed (Luke 22:41-42).	answers prayer (John 14:13-14).

said, The Father is greater than I (John 14:28).

did not know the day of final judgment (Mark 13:32).

died (John 19:30).

made himself equal with God (John 5:18).

accepted Peter's statement, Lord, you know everything (John 21:17).

raised Himself from the dead (John 10:18).

said, I am the resurrection and the life (John 11:25).

The following is a closer examination of some of the Biblical references to the deity of Jesus Christ.

In the beginning was the Word, and the Word was with God, and the Word was God (John 1:1).

The *New World Translation of the Holy Scriptures* (1970) used by the Jehovah's Witnesses translates the last clause of John 1:1, "The Word was a god." This translation—called grossly misleading by the Greek scholar Dr. Julius R. Mantey—is wrong for these reasons:

1. If the Watchtower translators had been consistent with the reasons they gave for translating "a god" in verse 1, they would have had to translate John 1:6 "There was a man sent from a god," John 1:12 "To all who received Him . . . He gave power to become children of a god," and John 1:18 "No one has ever seen a god." In other words, if Jesus is not God, then His Father is not God.

2. The translation "a god" conflicts with the first and foremost commandment, "You shall have no other gods before [or besides] Me" (Ex. 20:3). Jehovah God declares, "Besides Me there is no God" (Is. 44:6).

3. The Scriptures repeatedly describe Jesus as God, equal with His Father, by attributing to Him the same names and titles, the same honor, the same qualities, and the same acts as the Father. See the chapter "Jehovah Compared with Jesus Christ" for a fuller treatment of this subject.

My Lord and my God! (John 20:28). These words were spoken by Thomas to Jesus after His resurrection.

If Jesus is not God, He should have rebuked Thomas sharply as Peter (Acts 10:25-26), Barnabas and Paul (Acts 14:11-18), and the angel (Rev. 19:10; 22:8-9) reprimanded others who wanted to worship them. Yet Jesus commended Thomas.

Thou, Lord, didst found the earth in the beginning, and the heavens are the work of Thy hands (Heb. 1:10).

Who is the Creator of all things? God! Yet in Heb. 1:10 the Father Himself calls His Son the Creator of the heavens and the earth.

All things were made through Him, and without Him was not anything made that was made (John 1:3).

The inspired writer makes a distinction between the One who made and all things that were made. Jesus Christ is not one of the created things. He is the Creator, God. He is before—that is, He existed before—all things (Col. 1:17). All things were made through Jesus and in connection with Him.

Who then is this, that even wind and sea obey him? (Mark 4:41).

The awestruck people asked this question after Jesus had calmed the storm on the sea of Galilee. The answer is God. It is written in Ps. 89:9:

10

Thou [Lord God, verse 8] dost rule the raging of the sea; when its waves rise, thou stillest them.

Who can forgive sins but God alone? (Mark 2:7).

Christ's enemies angrily called Him a blasphemer when He forgave the sins of the paralytic (Mark 2:5). Yet Jesus claimed the authority only God has (Is. 43:25). To prove it He told the paralytic, "Rise . . . and walk" (Mark 2:9).

The Scriptures clearly teach that while Jesus Christ is true man, He is also true God.

He is called God.

He claims to be God.

He has the qualities of God.

He does the work of God.

Actually the marvel is not so much that Jesus is God but that the eternal Creator took the form of a servant that He might be our all-sufficient Savior.

3

Jehovah Compared with Jesus Christ

I am the Lord [Jehovah], that is My name; My glory I give to no other (Is. 42:8).

To whom will you liken Me and make Me equal, and compare Me, that We may be alike? (Is. 46:5).

The answer is no one. Yet there is One who is compared with the Lord [Jehovah] God again and again in the Scriptures. Some of the significant comparisons are:

Same names and titles

Jehovah	Jesus Christ
God said to Moses, "I am the *Lord*" (Ex. 6:2).	To what angel did God ever say, "Thou art My Son, today I have begotten Thee"? . . . And, "Thou, *Lord,* didst found the earth in the beginning, and the heavens are the work of Thy hands" (Heb. 1:5, 10).
I am *God,* and there is no other (Is. 45:22).	Thomas answered him, "My Lord and my *God!*" (John 20:28).
God said to Moses, "*I AM* WHO I AM" (Ex. 3:14).	Jesus said to them, " . . . before Abraham was, *I am*" (John 8:58).
A remnant will return, the remnant of Jacob, to the *mighty God* (Is. 10:21).	To us a Child is born, to us a Son is given...and His name will be called Wonderful Counselor, *Mighty God* (Is. 9:6).
This will be made manifest at the proper time by the blessed and only Sovereign, the *King of kings* and *Lord of lords* (1 Tim. 6:15).	He is clad in a robe dipped in blood ....On His robe and on His thigh he has a name inscribed, *King of kings* and *Lord of lords* (Rev. 19:13, 16).
I, I am the Lord, and besides Me there is no *Savior* (Is. 43:11).	They said to the woman, " . . . we know that this is indeed the *Savior* of the world" (John 4:42).
Behold, God is my *salvation* (Is. 12:2).	There is *salvation* in no one else, for there is no other name under heaven given among men by which we must be saved (Acts 4:12).
The Lord is my *Shepherd,* I shall not want (Ps. 23:1).	I am the good *Shepherd.* The good Shepherd lays down His life for the sheep (John 10:11).
For who is God, but the Lord? And who is a *Rock,* except our God? (Ps. 18:31).	They drank from the supernatural Rock which followed them, and the *Rock* was Christ (1 Cor. 10:4).
Thus says the Lord, the King of Israel and his Redeemer, the Lord of hosts: "I am *the First* and I am *the*	He laid His right hand upon me, saying, "Fear not, I am *the First and the Last,* and the living One; I

Last; besides Me there is no God (Is. 44:6).

I am *the Alpha and the Omega, the beginning and the end.* . . . and I will be his God and he shall be My son (Rev. 21:6, 7).

died, and behold I am alive for evermore (Rev. 1:17-18).

I am *the Alpha and the Omega,* the First and the Last, *the Beginning and the End.* . . . I Jesus have sent My angel to you with this testimony for the churches (Rev. 22:13, 16).

Worthy of the same honor

Thou art the Lord, Thou alone; Thou hast made heaven, the heaven of heavens, with all their hosts . . . and *the host of heaven worships Thee* (Neh. 9:6).

I am God, and there is no other. . . . To Me *every knee shall bow, every tongue shall swear* (Is. 45:22-23).

When He brings the Firstborn into the world, He says, "Let *all God's angels worship him"* (Heb. 1:6).

God has highly exalted Him and bestowed on Him the name which is above every name, that at the name of Jesus *every knee should bow,* in heaven and on earth and under the earth, and *every tongue confess* that Jesus Christ is Lord, to the glory of God the Father (Phil. 2:9-11).

Hallelujah! Salvation and *glory* and power belong to our God (Rev. 19:1).

To Him who loves us and has freed us from our sins by His blood . . . to Him be *glory* and dominion for ever and ever (Rev. 1:5-6).

Worthy art Thou, our Lord and God, *to receive* glory and honor and *power* (Rev. 4:11).

Worthy is the Lamb who was slain, *to receive power* and wealth and wisdom and might and honor and glory and blessing! (Rev. 5:12).

The people said to Joshua, *"The Lord our God we will serve* (Joshua 24:24).

"You are my witnesses," says the Lord (Is. 43:10).

You are serving the Lord Christ (Col. 3:24).

You shall be My witnesses (Acts 1:8).

Same qualities

Thy throne is established from *of old;* Thou art from *everlasting* (Ps. 93:2).

But you, O Bethlehem Ephrathah, . . . from you shall come forth for Me One who is to be ruler in Israel, whose origin is from *of old,* from ancient days (Micah 5:2).

His name will be called " . . . *Everlasting* Father, Prince of Peace" (Is. 9:6).

Jesus Christ is the *same yesterday and today and forever* (Heb. 13:8).

I the Lord *do not change* (Mal. 3:6).

I am God and not man, *the Holy*

You denied *the Holy* and Righteous

13

One in your midst (Hos. 11:9).

How *unsearchable* are His judgments and how inscrutable His ways! (Rom. 11:33).

Gracious is the Lord, and *righteous* (Ps. 116:5).

One (Acts 3:14).

This grace was given, to preach to the Gentiles the *unsearchable* riches of Christ (Eph. 3:8).

We have an advocate with the Father, Jesus Christ the *righteous* (1 John 2:1).

They said to Jeremiah, "May the Lord be a *true and faithful witness"* (Jer. 42:5).

God is our refuge and *strength* (Ps. 46:1).

The Lord is my *Light* and my Salvation (Ps. 27:1).

For Thou, O Lord, art my *Hope* (Ps. 71:5).

The words of the Amen, the *faithful and true witness,* the beginning of God's creation (Rev. 3:14).

I can do all things in Him who *strengthens* me (Phil. 4:13).

Jesus spoke to them, saying, "I am the *light* of the world" (John 8:12).

Paul, an apostle of Christ Jesus by command of God our Savior and of Christ Jesus our *Hope* (1 Tim. 1:1).

They have forsaken the Lord, the *fountain of living water* (Jer. 17:13).

The water that I shall give him will become in him a *spring of water welling up to eternal life* (John 4:14).

To the thirsty I will give from the fountain of the water of life (Rev. 21:6).

If any one thirst, let him *come to Me and drink* (John 7:37).

Same acts

In the beginning God *created the heavens and the earth* (Gen. 1:1).

Thou [My Son, Heb. 1:5], Lord, didst *found the earth* in the beginning, and the *heavens are the work of Thy hands* (Heb. 1:10).

Thou art the Lord, Thou alone; Thou hast made heaven, the heaven of heavens, with all their host, the earth and all that is on it, the seas and all that is in them; and Thou *preservest all of them* (Neh. 9:6).

He reflects the glory of God and bears the very stamp of His nature, *upholding the universe* by His word of power (Heb. 1:3).

O Israel, hope in the Lord! . . . And He will *redeem Israel from all his iniquities* (Ps. 130:7-8).

Awaiting our blessed hope, the appearing of the glory of our great God and Savior Jesus Christ, who gave Himself for us to *redeem us from all iniquity* (Titus 2:13-14).

I will *forgive* their iniquity, and I will remember their sin no more (Jer. 31:34).

When He saw their faith He said, "Man, your sins are *forgiven* you (Luke 5:20).

O Thou who *hearest prayer!* To Thee shall all flesh come (Ps. 65:2).

If you *ask* anything in My name, *I will do it* (John 14:14).

He *made the storm be still,* and the waves of the sea were hushed (Ps. 107:29).

He awoke and *rebuked the wind and the raging waves;* and they ceased, and *there was a calm* (Luke 8:24).

He is *wonderful in counsel,* and excellent in wisdom (Is. 28:29).

For to us a Child is born, to us a Son is given; . . . and His name will be called *"Wonderful Counselor"* (Is. 9:6).

God said, "I will *live in them* and move among them" (2 Cor. 6:16).

I have been crucified with Christ; it is no longer I who live, but Christ Who *lives in me* (Gal. 2:20).

Fear not, for *I am with you* (Is. 41:10).

I am with you always, to the close of the age (Matt. 28:20).

Thou, Thou only, *knowest the hearts* of all the children of men (1 Kings 8:39).

He knew all men and needed no one to bear witness of man; for He Himself *knew what was in man* (John 2:25).

God is greater than our hearts, and He *knows everything* (1 John 3:20).

Peter . . . said to him, "Lord, You *know everything;* You know that I love You" (John 21:17).

I the Lord *search* the mind and try the heart, to *give to every man according to his ways* (Jer. 17:10).

I am He who *searches* mind and heart, and I will *give to each of you as your works deserve* (Rev. 2:23).

You shall keep His statutes and His *commandments* (Deut. 4:40).

This I *command* you, to love one another (John 15:17).

The Lord *reproves him whom He loves* (Prov. 3:12).

Those whom I love, I reprove and chasten (Rev. 3:19).

No one is able to snatch them out of the Father's hand (John 10:29).

No one shall snatch them out of My hand (John 10:28).

If both you and the king who reigns over you will *follow the Lord your God,* it will be well. (1 Sam. 12:14).

He who *follows me* will not walk in darkness, but will have the light of life (John 8:12).

Behold, your God *will come with vengeance,* with the recompense of God (Is. 35:4).

When the Lord Jesus is revealed from heaven . . . *inflicting vengeance* upon those who do not know God and upon those who do not obey the gospel of our Lord Jesus (2 Thess. 1:7-8).

He will *judge* the world with righteousness (Psalm 96:13).

The Father judges no one, but has given all *judgment* to the Son (John 5:22).

Though a separate personality from the Father, Jesus Christ is true God. Therefore we are to worship and honor, love and obey God the Son as well as God the Father (John 5:23; Heb. 1:6).

4

Is It Right to Worship Jesus?

You shall worship the Lord your God and HIM only shall you serve (Matt. 4:10).

The Bible teaches that we are to worship God—and Him only. If Christ is a created being, worship of Him must be condemned as creature worship. Creature worship is an abomination in the eyes of the Lord. "They exchanged the truth about God for a lie and worshiped and served the creature rather than the Creator" (Rom. 1:25).

Angels Commanded to Worship Jesus

God the Father commands all the angels to worship Jesus (Heb. 1:6)— a direct quotation from the Septuagint (a Greek translation of the Old Testament): Worship Him [Jehovah], all ye His angels (Ps. 97:7). This command is so plain that it is impossible to refute it. Surely no one would suggest that this verse (Heb. 1:6) means only to worship THROUGH or IN THE NAME OF Jesus, for then to be consistent he would have to say that Ps. 97:7 means to worship THROUGH or IN THE NAME of Jehovah!

The Bible says, "Worship Him." The Bible means just that. But the New World Translation of the Watchtower Society has tried to eliminate mention of the worship paid to Jesus by using the words "do obeisance" instead of "worship." Heb. 1:6 is an example. Yet the same word for worship used in Heb. 1:6 appears in Rev. 22:8–9. The worship that the angel refused but told John to offer God is the same worship the Father commanded the angels to offer His Son in Heb. 1:6.

Those who say that only angels are commanded to worship Jesus have failed to see that *angels worship no one but God!* In Neh. 9:6 we learn that the host of heaven worships Jehovah. If angels worship Jesus (Heb. 1:6), it is simply because He is God. Certainly if angels, who are a higher creation than man (Heb. 2:7), must worship the Son, how much more are we required to worship Him! God does not have double standards. He does not permit creature worship in heaven or earth. When the Father says to anyone, be he angel or man, "Worship Him" (the Son), the Father is telling all who care to know the truth that His Son is the true God!

Worship or Obeisance?

Many times the Bible says that Christ was worshiped. The Greek word used for worship is *proskuneo*. This is the same word for worship used in Matt. 4:10, "You shall worship the Lord your God." The word is used, then, of true worship of God. Since this word (*proskuneo*) also means "do homage," how can we tell whether the worship paid to Jesus is simply homage or true worship due to God? God the Father answered this question for us in Heb. 1:6 by identifying the worship given to the Son as the same worship He Himself receives in Ps. 97:7! So the Father has sanctioned for the Son the same worship as for Himself.

A careful study of the worship given to Jesus will show also that in many cases this worship was accompanied by confession, prayer, adoration, and thanksgiving. Webster's definition of worship is "confession, adoration, prayer to, thanksgiving." So we have not only the word worship used in reference to Jesus, but the accompaniments of true worship as well.

Christ Accepts Worship

Our Lord Jesus Christ was sinless. He made no mistakes. He led no one astray. Yet He accepted worship of Himself. Peter refused worship of himself (Acts 10:26). The angel refused worship (Rev. 19:10; 22:9). But not once in all the cases where people worshiped Jesus did He ever refuse it, reprove them for doing it, or even suggest that it was sin. Yet to Satan He had said, "You shall worship the Lord your God and Him only shall you serve" (Matt. 4:10). Was Jesus a hypocrite? No. Was He guilty of the sin of Lucifer—wanting to be as the Most High? No. Did He accept worship to which He was not entitled? If we believe the Bible is true when it says that Jesus was without sin, then we know that Jesus accepted worship because He was entitled to it.

Truly He is the "Mighty God, Everlasting Father" (Is. 9:6). He was the "Lord and . . . God" of Thomas (John 20:28) as surely as Jehovah was the "God and . . . Lord" of David (Ps. 35:23).

Prayer—an Act of Worship

In Thayer's *Greek-English Lexicon* (p. 239) the expression "to call upon the name of the Lord" is defined "to invoke, adore, worship the Lord, that is, Christ." Just as the Hebrews called upon the name of Jehovah in the Old Testament in prayer, so in the New Testament the Christians call upon the name of Jesus. No one could fail to see that Jesus is invoked, adored, and worshiped all through the New Testament just the way in which Jehovah is invoked in the Old Testament. Even the New World Translation admits that Stephen prayed to Jesus in Acts 7:59, for it translates the Greek word *epikaleo* "invocation or prayer" in the footnote! *(The New World Translation of the Christian Greek Scriptures,* 1950, p. 377)

Prayer is to be made only to God. Each prayer to Jesus, then, was an act of true worship. Search your Bible for the many places it speaks of calling upon the name of Jesus. Always remember that it means "invoke, adore, worship."

. . . to bind all who call upon Thy name (Acts 9:14).

Is not this the man who made havoc in Jerusalem of those who called on this name? (Acts 9:21).

. . . all those who in every place call on the name of our Lord Jesus Christ (1 Cor. 1:2).

Each time we read that the Christians called upon the name of the Lord, they prayed to Him, they adored Him, they worshiped Him! Many prayers to Jesus are recorded in the Bible (1 Thess. 3:11; 2 Thess. 2:16-17; 1 Tim. 1:2; etc.). Yet we pray only to God, we adore only God, we worship only God. Truly Jesus is "our God and Savior Jesus Christ" (2 Peter 1:1).

Father and Son Receive Identical Worship

In Rev. 5:13 we see the magnificent sight of every creature everywhere worshiping God and the Lamb with identical worship. "To Him who sits upon the throne and to the Lamb be blessing and honor and glory and might for ever and ever!" In Is. 42:8 Jehovah had said, " . . . My glory I give to no other"—yet here we have the Father and Son sharing the same glory. "I and the Father are one" (John 10:30).

This worship in Rev. 5:13 is no display of creature worship. Creature worship is forbidden in the Bible. But Jesus is God (Is. 9:6). Jesus is the Creator (John 1:3). He founded the earth in the beginning (Heb. 1:10). He created all things in heaven and on earth (Col. 1:16). According to Jer. 10:10-11 the true God is the God who made the heavens and the earth.

O come, let us worship and bow down, let us kneel before the Lord, our Maker! (Ps. 95:6).

Christ to Be Worshiped as a Glorious Spirit?

The Watchtower book of doctrine teaches that Christ is "to be worshiped as a glorious spirit" *(Make Sure of All Things, 1953, p. 85)* But worship goes only to God! Regardless of how high a position they occupy, creatures are never to be worshiped. Some one might even suggest that only secondary worship is meant, but in this very book secondary worship is condemned (p. 177). Even bowing before men or angels is forbidden (p. 178). They do not mean obeisance to Christ or they would have said so, for they have been very careful to distinguish between worship and obeisance in their *New World Translation*. When it says worship, it means worship!

Even the charter of the Watchtower gives as one of its purposes the "public Christian worship of Almighty God *and* Christ Jesus." So once more they have identical worship given to God and Christ—who they say is a creature. Creature worship—an abomination to God!

Those who are forced to admit that the Bible teaches that Jesus is to be worshiped, yet scoff at the Bible teaching of the triune God, would do well to examine with unbiased mind the Bible teaching of the triune God. The Bible is not to be argued with, but to be delivered. We must believe the Bible when it calls Jesus "our great God and Savior Jesus Christ" (Titus 2:13).

We cannot refuse to believe what we cannot understand, for Jesus Himself said, "If I have told you earthly things and you do not believe how can you believe if I tell you heavenly things?" (John 3:12).

Christians Worship Christ as God the Son

True Christians are among those of whom Paul spoke: " . . . with all those who in every place call on the name of our Lord Jesus Christ" (1 Cor. 1:2). Let us join men, angels, and every created being to worship Him who created us—our Creator, our Savior, and the One who said, "Come to Me, all who labor and are heavy laden, and I will give you rest" (Matt. 11:28).

When they saw Him, they worshiped Him; but some doubted (Matt. 28:17). Let us be among those who worship Him—not among the doubters. If you do doubt, why not fall at His feet as Thomas did and cry, "My Lord and My God!" (John 20:28). Christ always hears the prayer of faith. And when you see Him in all His glory, you will know why John fell prostrate at the feet of Him who is "the First and the Last" (Rev. 1:17)—the ETERNAL ONE.

J. L. Jackson (used by permission)

5

The Resurrection of Jesus Christ Versus His Re-creation

The bodily resurrection of Jesus Christ is an essential truth of the Christian faith. Because our Lord rose bodily from the dead, we know that His sacrifice fully paid for our sins and that our own bodily resurrection is certain. The resurrected Christ told His disciples, "See My hands and My feet, that it is I myself; handle Me, and see; for a spirit has not flesh and bones as you see that I have (Luke 24:39).

Jesus made it clear that He was not a spirit creature. His resurrected body was the same body that had been nailed to the cross.

Jehovah's Witnesses claim they believe in the resurrection of Jesus. The truth, as the following dialogue demonstrates, is that they deny this central Bible teaching.

Christian: Do you believe in the resurrection?

Jehovah's
Witness: Why, of course, I do. The Bible teaches it, and we certainly believe the Bible.

Christian: I'm glad to know that. It gives us an authority. If you believe it, and we believe it, then we can refer to it during our discussion.

Jehovah's
Witness: Not every so-called Christian accepts the Bible today. In fact, Jehovah's Witnesses lead the way today in accepting it as the Word of God.

C To get back to the resurrection—I read in your *Let God Be True* book (1952) that some people after Jesus' death tried to "thwart the Son of God's coming forth from the grave." (p. 273—274)

JW That's true. They were the religious leaders of that day, too.

C I take it then that you believe He did come from the grave?

JW He certainly did. The resurrection is a foundation stone of the Bible.

C When you speak of "he" coming forth from the grave, do you mean Jesus?

JW Of course. That's a strange question, especially since I just said I believe he came out.

C Please forgive me if I seem to be working over this too much. But it's a terribly important point. Do you agree with Paul that if Christ has not been raised, you faith is futile? (1 Cor. 15:17)

JW Of course.

C Now when Christ rose from the grave as you said you believe, did His body rise?

JW Oh no. His body didn't rise. We don't know what happened to his body. Likely Jehovah dissolved it in gases . . . maybe He even hid it. But it didn't rise.

C   Well, if Jesus' body didn't rise, was it His soul that rose from the grave?

JW Of course not. The soul and the body are the same thing. There is no soul separate and distinct from the body. It tells us that in our *Make Sure of All Things* (1953, p. 349).

C   Please bear with me if I seem to be a bit in a fog. You say you believe Jesus rose, yet you don't believe His body or His soul rose. Then you must believe His spirit rose. Do you not?

JW His spirit was just his breath. It didn't rise!

C   If neither His body, soul, or spirit rose—WHAT did?

JW Why, he did.

C   What was the HE? Is there a part of us that isn't body, soul, or spirit?

JW No, I guess not. Actually he didn't rise, he was re-created a spirit.

C   But I thought you said you believed in the resurrection.

JW I do. Jesus was re-created.

C   But re-creation isn't resurrection.

JW Of course, it is. God holds you in his memory. Then he creates someone with your life pattern.

C   Then it isn't *you* that rises—I'm sorry, that is re-created. It's your identical twin.

JW Oh no, it's YOU.

C   Well, was it Jesus who rose?

JW The man Jesus is buried forever. Christ is now a glorious spirit in heaven.

C   Then you don't believe Jesus rose. You don't believe in the resurrection at all. Why did Jesus show His body to Thomas?

JW He just assumed a body so the disciples would believe in his resurrection.

C   You mean He assumed a body with nail prints in the hands and feet to convince the disciples that it was the same body, therefore the same Jesus?

JW Well, yes, I guess so.

C   Then you really believe Jesus was a deceiver—to assume a body which didn't exist to prove He rose when He didn't!

JW Our books teach us that. Our books are always true.

C   Now I have a few questions for you. First, your books say that religious men tried to thwart the Son of God's coming forth from the grave. Now if nothing came from the grave anyway as you teach, what were they trying to thwart?

JW I never thought of that.

C   Your *Let God Be True* book also says that the resurrection is "no illusion or imagined thing" (p. 273). In other words, your book means to say that the resurrection actually happened. No one just imagined it. Yet you admit that it didn't take place at all. Which would make it an illusion!

JW An illusion?

C   Yes. Your *Let God Be True* book also says that Satan and his demons tried to obscure the true meaing of the resurrection by teaching that the resurrection was only in a spiritual sense (p. 274). Yet you teach that Jesus' resurrection did not really take place. It was a spiritual resurrection! Now what kind of double talk is your book using?

JW There must be an answer. I will write the Watchtower.

C Why write them? You have in your books what they teach. Now another question. Your book talks about the grave being emptied (*Let God Be True,* p. 282). If nothing comes out of the grave, why do you talk about the grave being emptied?

JW That's what the Bible says.

C I know. It says people will come out of their graves. The graves will be opened because according to Bible resurrection the body rises! When Lazarus was raised from the dead, did his body rise?

JW I guess it did.

C When the widow's son was raised, did his body rise?

JW Yes.

C In every resurrection in the Bible the body rose, didn't it? And when Jesus spoke of His own death as a resurrection, He said, Destroy this temple, and in three days I will raise it up (John 2:19). He spoke of the temple of His BODY (John 2:21). How much clearer could the Bible be?

JW But Watchtower says he didn't rise. How can I tell what is truth?

C Follow the Bible. Search the Scriptures. You have let men tell you what to believe instead of believing the Bible. And you have gone further. You claim to believe the Bible while you reject the simplest thing it teaches. And remember, the Bible says, If Christ has not been raised, your faith is futile and you are still in your sins (1 Cor. 15:17).

(This dialogue has been used effectively by both youth and adult groups.)

6

One God—Three Divine Personalities

The word "Trinity" is made up of two Latin words—*tri,* meaning three, and *unus,* meaning one. It is not found in the Bible but is used to indicate the three Personalities in God. The point is not whether the word "Trinity" appears in the Bible. The fact is that God has revealed Himself in Scriptures as God the Father, God the Son, and God the Holy Spirit.

It is not a question whether such a teaching is reasonable or understandable. We cannot fully understand a blade of grass or the microscopic atom. So God is far beyond our reason and understanding. Nor is it a question of whether the Nicene Creed (325 A.D.) and the Athanasian Creed (5th or 6th century) uphold the Trinity doctrine. Our faith rests on divine Scriptures, not on human creeds. Ancient pagans may have worshiped trinities of gods. Their perverted belief does not make the Trinity a pagan error any more than the heathen practice of prayer makes all prayer wrong. The decisive question is: What do the inspired Scriptures say?

Jehovah's Witnesses answer: "What, then, do the facts show as to the Trinity? Neither the word nor the idea is in God's Word, the Bible." *(The Truth That Leads to Eternal Life,* 1968, p. 25)

> May the Lord open our minds to understand
> His Word as we examine the Bible and the
> interpretation of the Watchtower.

The Bible from beginning to end consistently teaches there is only one God. In Deut. 6:4 we read: "Hear, O Israel: The Lord our God is one Lord." The Hebrew word "one" used here is most significant. It is not *yachid,* which means "the only one." (Example: In Gen. 22:2 God said to Abraham. "Take your son, your only son Isaac, . . . and offer him.") The Hebrew word in Deut. 6:4 is *echad,* which means unity or united one. (Examples: Gen. 1:5, There was evening and there was morning, one day. Gen. 2:24, A man leaves his father and his mother and cleaves to his wife, and they become one flesh.) It is evident that the writer of Deut. 6:4 means to indicate that God is a united one. The obvious implication is that there is more than one Person in the one God.

It is clear to all that the Father is God. But Jehovah's Witnesses hold that Jesus is not God. According to their belief Jesus was at first an angel. Then for thirty-three years He lived as a man on earth. Now He is an angel again in heaven. They insist that He was never equal with His Father.

Their *New World Translation of the Holy Scriptures* translates John 1:1, "In (the) beginning the Word was, and the Word was with God, and the Word was a god." In other words, Jehovah's Witnesses believe: Jesus Christ, a god, was with God. But Jehovah God absolutely rejects this interpretation of Scriptures when He declares, "Before Me no God was formed, nor shall there be any after Me" (Is. 43:10), and "There is no other God besides me" (Is. 45:21).

But, say Jehovah's Witnesses, does not 1 Cor. 8:5 state, "There are many 'gods'"? True! Satan is called the "god of this world" (2 Cor. 4:4). To the judges in the Old Testament period God said, "You are gods, sons of the Most High" (Ps. 82:6). But Satan is a false object of worship. The judges were agents of God, not God Himself. Of them it was written, "You shall die like men and fall like any prince" (Ps. 82:7). Jesus, on the other hand, is truly God.

The apostle Paul states, "You are serving the Lord Christ" (Col. 3:24). Did he mean they were serving just another man? No, for the apostle writes that they were serving "the Lord and not men" (Col. 3:23). Were they serving a god? No. We must serve God alone. Stephen prayed, "Lord Jesus, receive my spirit" (Acts 7:59). Was he praying to a god? That would have been idolatry. Prayer is to be directed only to God.

If the Father is God and Jesus is God, are there two Gods? No. God, as Deut. 6:4 states, is a unity. God is so complete, so absolute, that He cannot be divided into two or three.

Jesus Christ said, "I and the Father are one" (John 10:30). Does the word "one" in this statement describe nothing more than Jesus' complete harmony of will and purpose with His Father? The immediate context teaches otherwise. Jesus as man had just declared, "My Father . . . is greater than all" (John 10:29). Yet as God in human form He claimed the same divine power as His Father. He said that no one could snatch His sheep out of either His hand or that of His Father (John 10:28-29). Then He said, "I and the Father are one" (John 10:30). Immediately the unbelieving "Jews took up stones again to stone Him" (John 10:31). Why? They answered: "We stone you . . . because you, being a man, make yourself God" (John 10:33).

In John 17:22 Jesus prayed that His followers "may be one even as we [Father and Son] are one." He further prayed that the unity of the believers might be demonstrated in love, so that the world might know that the Father sent Jesus (John 17:21, 23). How was the oneness of Christ's people to be achieved? Jesus answers: "I in them and thou in Me" (John 17:23). As the Father dwells in the Son, so Jesus dwells in those who open their hearts to Him. Through the Christ who dwells in them, His people become one— one body (Eph. 4:4). The oneness of John 17:22 therefore refers to the oneness of believers through the indwelling Christ. The oneness Jesus claims in John 10:30 is equality with His Father.

No one has ever seen God (John 1:18). God says, "You cannot see My face; for man shall not see Me and live" (Ex. 33:20). No sinful human can bear the sight of God in all His glory. Yet Jesus has seen God. In fact, Jesus has existed in the bosom of the Father, in the closest possible intimacy with His Father (John 1:18). He is the only begotten (literal translation of the Greek word *monogenes*) Son of the Father (John 3:16). A man creates or makes a tool—something different from himself. A man begets a son—of the same nature as the man. So the only begotten Son of God is of the same nature as His eternal Father. The Son has made known the Father to us because He has lived in the closest possible relation with His Father. The Son of God told Philip, "He who has seen Me has seen the Father" (John 14:9). To see Jesus with the eyes of faith is to see God Himself, for Jesus, as He stood before Philip, was truly God in human form. Of Him the apostle wrote, "In him the whole fulness of deity dwells bodily" (Col. 2:9).

When Jesus the man referred to His Father, He called Him "My God," as He did on the cross (Matt. 27:46) and after His resurrection (John 20:17).

In John 17:3 Jesus the man prays to His Father, saying, "This is eternal life, that they know Thee the only true God, and Jesus Christ whom Thou hast sent." In this statement Jesus makes Himself one and equal with His Father. He declares that to receive eternal life we must know by experience the Son as well as the Father. Can a creature—whether perfect man or holy angel—give eternal life? No. It is only for God to give. Jesus said, "I give them [My sheep] eternal life" (John 10:28).

What is the relation of Jesus as God to His Father? Paul states, "The head of Christ is God" (1 Cor. 11:3). Christ's submission to His Father's will in no way implies that He as God is unequal with His Father. The head of a woman is her husband (1 Cor. 11:3). Yet the woman shares the same nature as the man. So in the triune God there is willing submission of the Son to the Father. Yet the Father and the Son are equally God. The Son shares the same divine form or nature as His Father (Phil. 2:6), for the fullness of God's being is in His Son (Col. 2:9).

1 Cor. 15:28 states, "When all things are subjected to Him, then the Son Himself will also be subjected to Him who put all things under Him, that God may be everything to every one." When the world was created, Christ became "the Firstborn [Head, Ps. 89:27] of all creation" (Col. 1:15). Satan corrupted God's creation. But Jesus by His death and resurrection has dethroned the devil as the ruler of this world. While the devil still causes much havoc, he is the defeated enemy of God. At His final coming Jesus Christ will clinch His victory over Satan. Then the victorious Christ will lay His work as mankind's Savior, complete and perfect, into His Father's hand. In this act of subjection He will submit Himself and His whole creation to God the Father. Then God—the Father, Son, and Spirit—will manage all creation.

> The Bible thus teaches that the Father is God,
> and the Son is true God and true man.
> The Bible also teaches the reality of the Holy Spirit.

To Jehovah's Witnesses the Holy Spirit is nothing more than God's invisible, active force. *(Let God Be True,* 1952, p. 108). They claim that the Holy Spirit cannot be a person, for John the Baptist said that Jesus would baptize with the Holy Spirit and with fire (Matt. 3:11). How, ask Jehovah's Witnesses, can one person baptize with another person?

On Pentecost Peter quoted Joel 2:28, "I will pour out my Spirit on all flesh" (Acts 2:17). Jehovah's Witnesses regard this statement as further evidence that the Holy Spirit cannot be a person. Again they demonstrate their inability to distinguish between figurative and literal language, and their reliance on human reason instead of the Holy Scriptures. Job asks, "Didst Thou not pour me out like milk?" (Job 10:10). It is quite obvious that it is Scriptural to refer to a person as being poured out.

Jehovah's Witnesses try to prove that the Holy Spirit is an "it," not a person. It is written, Rom. 8:16 (King James Version), "The Spirit Itself beareth witness with our spirit" (The Revised Standard Version translates "The Spirit Himself".) The word "Spirit" in Greek is *pneuma,* a neuter noun. It is grammatically proper for the neuter noun to be followed by the neuter pronoun "itself." However, this does not disprove the personality of the Holy Spirit. In John 4:24 it is stated, "God is spirit." Yet God is not an "it."

John 16:13 speaks of the Holy Spirit as "the Spirit [*pneuma*] of truth." Yet the neuter word *pneuma* is referred to by *ekeinos,* the masculine form of the Greek pronoun meaning "he." Therefore even the *New World Translation of the Holy Scriptures* (1970) has to render John 16:13, "However, when that one arrives, the spirit of truth, he will guide you into all truth, for he will not speak of his own impulse, but what things he hears he will speak, and he will declare to you the things coming." In John 16 the *New World Translation of the Holy Scriptures* (1970) refers to the Holy Spirit (translated "helper" or "the spirit of the truth") 10 times as a person ("he," "his," or "him").

The marks of a personality are intellect, emotion, and will. An impersonal force cannot teach. The Holy Spirit does. Jehovah's Witnesses say the Holy Spirit may be likened to a radar beam. A radar beam cannot love or be grieved. The Holy Spirit can. An invisible force cannot forbid. The Holy Spirit does.

The Holy Spirit

speaks, calls	The Holy Spirit said, "Set apart for Me [note the personal pronoun] Barnabas and Saul for the work to which I have called them (Acts 13:2).
hears	The Spirit of truth . . . will not speak on His own authority, but whatever He hears He will speak (John 16:13).
teaches	The Holy Spirit, whom the Father will send in My name, He will teach you all things (John 14:26).
counsels	I will pray the Father, and He will give you another Counselor, to be with you forever, even the Spirit of truth (John 14:16-17).
knows the future	Thus says the Holy Spirit, "So shall the Jews at Jerusalem bind the man who owns this girdle and deliver him into the hands of the Gentiles" (Acts 21:11).
forbids	They went through the region of Phrygia and Galatia, having been forbidden by the Holy Spirit to speak the word in Asia (Acts 16:6).
may be lied to	Ananias, why has Satan filled your heart to lie to the Holy Spirit . . . ? (Acts 5:3).
may be grieved	Do not grieve the Holy Spirit of God (Eph. 4:30).
intercedes	The Spirit intercedes for the saints according to the will of God (Rom. 8:27).
loves	I appeal to you . . . by the love of the Spirit. (Rom. 15:30).

Only a personality can do what the Holy Spirit does. The Bible clearly speaks of the Holy Spirit as a person. The Bible also teaches that the Spirit is God.

In the first church at Jerusalem Ananias and his wife Sapphira sold some property and brought only part of the money to the apostles, claiming it was the full price. But Peter said, "Ananias, why has Satan filled your heart to lie to the Holy Spirit and to keep back part of the proceeds of the land?" Peter went on to identify the Holy Spirit. He explained in the next verse: "You have not lied to men but to God" (Acts 5:3-4). Peter leaves no doubt about the matter: The Holy Spirit is God.

The Holy Spirit is identified in the Scriptures with the Lord (Jehovah). The Lord told the prophet Isaiah, "Go, and say to this people: 'Hear and hear, but do not understand; see and see, but do not perceive'" (Is. 6:9). In Acts 28:25-26 the apostle Paul states that it was the Holy Spirit who spoke these words through Isaiah. The Jews in the desert put the Lord (Jehovah) to the proof (Ex. 17:2). In Heb. 3:9 the Holy Spirit says, "Your fathers put Me to the test." In Jeremiah 31:33 the Lord (Jehovah) declares, "I will put My law within them." In Heb. 10:16 the Holy Spirit says, "I will put My laws on their hearts."

Thus there are three Persons mentioned in the Scriptures who share equally the divine name of God. It is in their divine name that we are to be baptized—in the name of the Father, Son, and Holy Spirit (Matt. 28:19).

Again and again the Bible differentiates between the Father, Son, and Spirit. While the Scriptures ascribe specific works to each of the three Persons in the Godhead, all Persons share in the work of each. The following are examples:

There is "one Lord" (Eph. 4:5). Jesus prays to the "Father, Lord of heaven and earth" (Matt. 11:25). James 2:1 speaks of "Jesus Christ, the Lord of glory," and 2 Cor. 3:17 states, "The Lord is the Spirit."

There is "one Spirit" (Eph. 4:4). He is "the Holy Spirit" (Matt. 28:19), "the Spirit of Christ" (Rom. 8:9), and "the Spirit of Him who raised Jesus from the dead" (Rom. 8:11).

The Spirit creates (Ps. 104:30). The Son of God is the Creator (Heb. 1:10). The Father made all things (1 Cor. 8:6). The one God created us (Mal. 2:10).

The Spirit of God dwells in you (Rom. 8:9). Christ dwells in your hearts (Eph. 3:17). The Father and the Son make their home in the man of Christ (John 14:23). God dwells in His temple, His people (2 Cor. 6:16).

Clearly the teaching of God as a tri-unity is not "another of Satan's attempts to keep God-fearing persons from learning the truth of Jehovah and His Son Jesus Christ" (*Let God Be True,* 1952, p. 111). It is rather the positive testimony of Scriptures.

The truth of Scriptures is:

There are three distinct divine Persons.

These three Personalities are equal in their characteristics, but they are one Being.

They are properly called God, whether separately or collectively.

They are not three separate Gods, but only one eternal God—Father, Son, and Spirit.

7

Salvation

What must I do to be saved? This is life's crucial question. The apostle Paul answers: "Believe in the Lord Jesus, and you will be saved" (Acts 16:31). It is also written, "God so loved the world that He gave His only Son, that whoever believes in Him should not perish but have eternal life" (John 3:16).

Scriptures clearly teach that we are saved from dying unforgiven in our sins and receive eternal life by putting our complete trust in Jesus Christ, whom the Father gave as a sacrifice in our place.

What does the Watchtower teach? The following statements appear in *"Make Sure of All Things"* (1965, pp. 438—439): "Salvation possible only through faith in Jesus Christ. Salvation not earned so that it is due us; an expression of God's undeserved kindness."

At first glance it would seem that Jehovah's Witnesses interpret the Bible correctly. Other declarations, however, reveal that their teaching is totally different from that of Christ and the apostles. Let's compare what the Jehovah's Witnesses really teach about salvation with the Bible.

Jehovah's Witness	Bible

Was Christ's death a human or a divine-human sacrifice?

He (the Son of God) came . . . to die as a human sacrifice for all mankind, that we might have life eternal *(Things in Which It Is Impossible for God to Lie,* 1965, p. 219).	In Him (Jesus Christ) the whole fulness of deity dwells bodily (Col. 2:9). He Himself bore our sins in His body on the tree (1 Peter 2:24).
Comment: According to Jehovah's Witnesses Christ sacrificed nothing more than a human body.	Since God in His fulness dwells in Jesus' human body, Jesus made a divine-human sacrifice, not a simple human sacrifice.

Did Christ give His life as a ransom for Adam only or for all people?

The perfect justice of God would not unjustly accept more value than that of the thing to be ransomed. . . . It was the perfect man Adam that had sinned and so had lost for his offspring human perfection and its privileges. Jesus must likewise be humanly perfect, to correspond with the sinless Adam in Eden. In that way he could offer a ransom	Who [the man Christ Jesus] gave himself as a ransom for all (1 Tim. 2:6). He died for all (2 Cor. 5:15). Adam's sin was so great that it brought death to all men (Rom. 5:12). When Jesus died, He was on the one side of the balance; the whole world was on the other side.

27

that exactly corresponded in value with what the sinner Adam lost for his descendants. This requirement of divine justice did not allow for Jesus to be more than a perfect man (*Things in Which It Is Impossible for God to Lie,* 1965, p. 232). Comment: On the one hand, Jehovah's Witnesses say that Jesus died for all mankind. Yet they limit the value of Christ's ransom and belittle the immensity of His work of atonement.

They claim that Christ was no more than a perfect man. So they teach that His atonement was the case of one perfect human life being given to redeem another human life. They maintain that Jesus gave His life as a ransom for Adam only.

Because the whole fullness of deity dwells bodily in Jesus (Col. 2:9), His death was of infinite value. He died in the place of not just one sinner but all sinners. He gave His life as a ransom for all, not for Adam only.

Is salvation only a future possibility or a present reality?

The marvelous prospect of eternal life under the righteous kingdom of God awaits the survivors of the end of this wicked system of things (p. 101). The initial program of the Kingdom will cover a period of one thousand years (p. 106). When paradise is restored to earth, Jesus will again use his power to raise the dead (p. 109). Those resurrected to life on earth will come forth to the opportunity of gaining eternal life in paradise (p. 110). By the close of the first thousand years it (that is, God's kingdom by Christ) . . . will have removed every trace of unrighteousness. All humankind on earth will stand as perfect creatures before the throne of the Supreme Judge, Jehovah God. . . . Jehovah will give them the opportunity to show their loyalty. How? By releasing Satan and his demons from their condition of restraint in the "abyss" (Rev. 20:7). . . . Those who stay loyal to God will be judged worthy of everlasting life *(The*

He who believes in the Son has eternal life (John 3:36).

He who hears My word and believes Him who sent Me, has eternal life; he does not come into judgment, but has passed from death to life (John 5:24).

I write this to you who believe in the name of the Son of God, that you may know that you have eternal life (1 John 5:13).

. . . that I may gain Christ and be found in Him, not having a righteousness of my own, based on law, but that which is through faith in Christ, the righteousness from God that depends on faith (Phil. 3:8-9).

Christ, having been offered once to bear the sins of many, will appear a second time, not to deal with sin but to save those who are eagerly waiting for him (Heb. 9:28).

By his life, death, and resurrection

28

Truth That Leads to Eternal Life, 1968, pp. 112—113).

Comment: Jehovah's Witnesses cannot be sure they are saved now, for they do not trust in the finished work of Jesus. Even after the resurrection they can only look forward to the opportunity of proving themselves worthy of everlasting life.

Jesus did more than give us an opportunity to receive everlasting life. He completely delivered us from the guilt and eternal consequences of our sins.

Our salvation is a present reality. We have eternal life now. We are declared righteous and justified in this present life.

At the same time our salvation is not yet wholly realized. Salvation in its full and final sense will be accomplished at Christ's final coming. Then we will be completely delivered from the presence and power of sin.

Are we saved by faith plus good works or through faith in Jesus alone?

The way to heavenly life involves more than just faith in Christ's ransom sacrifice and works of faith in obedience to God's instructions. ...This (calling and choosing by God through His Son) involves a number of steps or actions taken to qualify such a one for the heavenly inheritance, many of such steps being taken by God, others by the one called *(Aid to Bible Understanding,* 1971, p. 735).

We have to do more than merely accept the Kingdom message in order to be saved. We also have to preach it in order to show that we believe it. We are saved by more than just believing the Kingdom message with all our hearts; we must also publicly declare that Kingdom message to others *(From Paradise Lost to Paradise Regained,* 1958, p. 249).

Because Jesus had God as His Father, he was a perfect man. As a perfect man he had the right to life. By willingly laying down his human life he could use its right to buy back the worthy ones of

By grace you have been saved through faith; and this is not your own doing, it is the gift of God—not because of works, lest any man should boast (Eph. 2:8-9).

They are justified by His grace as a gift, through the redemption which is in Christ Jesus (Rom. 3:24).

Our good works do not save us. Everlasting life is not due to any worthiness on our part. Our salvation is an undeserved gift of God. We cannot remove our guilt by our obedience. Jesus' blood alone cleanses us from all sin (1 John 1:7).

Witnessing to our Savior, like love of the brethren and a forgiving spirit, are proofs of a saving faith. Jesus alone saves, not Jesus and our good works.

Adam's children *(From Paradise Lost to Paradise Regained,* 1958, p. 143).

Comment: Jehovah's Witnesses teach that faith in Christ's sacrifice is not sufficient for salvation. Such works as study, using Watchtower publications, attending meetings, and door-to-door witnessing are necessary to be saved.

Is the new birth necessary only for some or for all?

Being born again, begotten as spiritual sons of God, necessary for those who would enter the heavenly kingdom of God *(Make Sure of All Things,* 1965, p. 56).

Comment: Jehovah's Witnesses say that the other sheep—who according to their belief will live forever not in heaven but on the new earth after the resurrection—need not and cannot be born again.

Truly, truly, I say to you, unless one is born anew, he cannot see the kingdom of God (John 3:3).

All who enter Christ's kingdom must be born again.

Will only 144,000 people enter heaven?

Rev. 14:1-3 says that 144,000 followers will be with the Lamb Jesus Christ on the heavenly Mount Zion. These are the only ones whom Jehovah God takes to heaven with his Son. All others who gain life in His new world will live in paradise restored here on earth *(From Paradise Lost to Paradise Regained,* 1958, p. 153).

The Bible plainly shows that some of these, that is, 144,000, will share in heavenly glory with Christ Jesus, while the others will enjoy the blessings of life down here on earth *(Let God Be True,* 1952, p. 298).

Comment: The Watchtower restricts heaven to only 144,000 people.

After this I looked, and behold, a great multitude which no man could number, from every nation [note: not just from the Jewish nation], from all tribes and peoples and tongues, standing before the throne and before the Lamb (Rev. 7:9).

A countless number of followers of Jesus—not just 144,000—will be in heaven before the throne of God and His son.

Then I looked, and lo, on Mount Zion stood the Lamb, and with Him a hundred and forty-four thousand who had His name and His Father's name written on their foreheads.... It is these who have not defiled themselves with women, for they are chaste; it is these who follow the Lamb wherever He goes; these have been redeemed from mankind as first fruits for God and the Lamb (Rev. 14:1, 4).

And I heard the number of the

sealed, a hundred and forty-four thousand sealed, out of every tribe of the sons of Israel (Rev. 7:4).

If these words are taken literally, the only people who will appear before the heavenly throne are 12,000 male Jews from each of the 12 tribes who have never had sexual relations with women. Rev. 14:4, however, states that the 144,-000 are not the total number of believers in Jesus who will enter heaven. They are only the first fruits, the first of a much larger number to follow.

Are there two classes of Christians— the 144,000 and the other sheep?

So the 144,000 are persons who die on earth as humans and are resurrected to heavenly life as spirit creatures, as Jesus was (Rom. 6:5). When compared with the thousands of millions of persons who live on earth, they are, indeed, a "little flock." However, the "little flock" who go to heaven are not the only ones who receive salvation. As we have seen, they will have happy earthly subjects. Jesus referred to these as his "other sheep," of whom "a great crowd" are even now serving God faithfully (John 10:16; Rev. 7:9, 15) *(The Truth That Leads to Eternal Life,* 1968, p. 77).

Comment: The Watchtower teaches that there are two classes of Christians: (1) The heavenly class. They are the kingdom of God that supposedly began in 1914. They rule over the earthly class *(Make Sure of All Things,* 1953, p. 231). (2) The earthly class. They don't have to be born again. They will be raised to live on earth and will be ruled by Christ and his 144,000 "associate kings."

Fear not, little flock, for it is your Father's good pleasure to give you the kingdom (Luke 12:32).

In this instance, Jesus was speaking to His disciples. They were a little band compared with the entire Jewish nation. So Christ's true followers today—even though they are much larger in number than when Christ was on earth in the flesh—are still only a small minority in the world.

I have other sheep, that are not of this fold; I must bring them also, and they will heed my voice. so there shall be one flock, one shepherd (John 10:16).

Christ's other sheep were the Gentiles, who were not part of God's ancient people. The Gentile believers together with the Jewish believers—two folds—would become one flock.

Jesus does not differentiate between a heavenly and earthly class of followers. He gives eternal life to all His sheep (John 10:28). The countless followers of the Lamb, who is also the Shepherd, will be in heaven before the throne of God and with Jesus (Rev. 7:9-10).

31

Though Jehovah's Witnesses speak of Jesus as the Savior and of salvation as the free gift of God, they believe that Jesus' death was nothing more than a human sacrifice— for Adam's sin only—and that salvation is dependent in part on what man does.

While true believers in Jesus are certain of their salvation in this present life, Jehovah's Witnesses believe that salvation offers only an opportunity after the resurrection to receive eternal life.

Jehovah's Witnesses dishonor Christ, denying His deity, and thus deprive themselves of the eternal salvation He came to bring.

8

Witnessing to Jehovah's Witnesses

Jehovah's Witnesses who come to your door are a God-given opportunity. You have something wonderful to offer them—a personal relation to a living Savior instead of to an organization. How can you share the Good News effectively with them?

1. *Ask the Holy Spirit to give you wisdom* to declare and defend the truth with power. Keep in mind that when you deal with Jehovah's Witnesses you are confronting people under the influence of Satan, a master of twisting Scriptures.

2. *Pray that your heart will be filled with love* for Jehovah's Witnesses. Tell them that you love them and will pray for them. Continue to pray that they may welcome Jesus into their lives as Savior and Lord.

3. *Witness boldly and joyfully.* Tell what Jesus means to you—how much He loves you, how He has changed your life, that through faith in Him you know you have eternal life now.

* * *

Concentrate on the basic issue, the deity of Jesus Christ.

Stick to one subject. Don't jump from one topic to another.

Encourage Jehovah's Witnesses to put aside all Watchtower literature and to study God's Word only. Urge them to pray, "God, I will believe whatever You want me to believe."

Do not let Jehovah's Witnesses take charge of the discussion. Take the initiative.

Discuss Bible verses in their context, in the light of the surrounding verses.

Don't ridicule. Never argue.

Use a reliable Bible translation such as the New International Version, the Revised Standard Version, or the King James Version.

Have a set of cards readily available noting the passages where Jesus and Jehovah God share the same names, works, and qualities. Use these cards when Jehovah's Witnesses come to the door.

Cross reference your Bible. Make brief notes in it. Keep a notebook to record parallel verses, explanations, etc.

Definitions

Jehovah's Witnesses claim to believe in Jesus as Savior, in hell, everlasting life, etc. But they fill these words and concepts with false meaning. Here are definitions of certain important terms from their book *"Make Sure of All Things"* (1953).

Death—termination of existence (p. 86).

Divine life—life of the highest order, like that of the Divine Being, Jehovah God himself. Reserved only for Christ Jesus and his 144,000

Kingdom-ruling associates. No others besides the Kingdom members in heaven receive incorruptibility and immortality (p. 243).

Everlasting death—annihilation (pp. 330—331).

Everlasting life—life in a perfect organism, fleshly for humans who gain life on earth, spiritual for faithful angels who continue to live in heaven (p. 243).

Faith—true Christian faith is the sum of beliefs concerning Jehovah God and his Kingdom (p. 119).

Hell—common grave of mankind (p. 155).

Holy Spirit—active force (p. 360).

Incarnation—a clothing, or state of being clothed, with flesh; taking on, or being manifested in, a body of flesh. Scripturally, it describes the conditions of angels appearing to mankind on earth (p. 179).

Jehovah—greatest Personality in the universe, Creator, not triune (p. 188); not omnipresent (p. 191).

Jesus Christ—a created individual; Michael the Archangel (pp. 207, 150).

Kingdom of God—the capital or ruling part of God's universal organization. It is comprised of the King Christ Jesus and 144,000 associate kings taken from among men. It is entirely heavenly, having no earthly part. All becoming members must be resurrected and given spirit bodies. Kingdom began operation in full power with the enthronement of Christ in the heavens A. D. 1917 (p. 226). All selected for Kingdom must die in order to enter it (p. 235).

Man of lawlessness—the collective clergy of Christendom (p. 14).

Resurrection—a restoration to life of the nonexistent dead (p. 311).

Soul—a living creature; a human does not possess a soul separate and distinct from the body (p. 349).

Trinity—a false, unbiblical doctrine (p. 386).

Using the Scriptures with Jehovah's Witnesses

Insist that they be consistent. Example: They say that the "Word" in John 1:1 is "a god," a created person. Have them write down each verse of this chapter substituting "a god" each time the "Word" is referred to. Try it yourself. Example—John 1:3: "All things were made through a god [a creature]." Compare this with what the Scriptures say: "The builder of all things is God" (Heb. 3:4); "I am the Lord, who made all things. . . . Who was with me?" (Is. 44:24). The Lord (Jehovah) declares that He created all things by Himself, alone.

Make their strong verses your strong verses. Jehovah's Witnesses try to paralyze your strongest proof texts. For example, they maintain that the term "the Firstborn of all creation" (Col. 1:15), which is applied to Christ, proves He is a creature. "Firstborn" sometimes does mean the first one born. At other times it means the first in rank, position, or privilege—the heir. Examples: "Joseph called the name of the first-born Manasseh. . . . The name of the second he called Ephraim" (Gen. 41:51-52). Yet it is written, "I am a Father to Israel, and Ephraim is My first-born" (Jer. 31:9). Why is Jesus called the Firstborn of all creation in Col. 1:15? The answer is given in the next verse: "in Him all things were created." Jesus is the Firstborn not because he was the first one born but because He is the Creator.

If you know Greek, you have an advantage. Note how the Watchtower translators made their *New World Translation* prove their doctrines. They omitted the word "now" in Rom. 8:1 ("There is therefore now no condemnation for those who are in Christ Jesus"). Why did they omit "now"? Answer: They do not believe in a present salvation. Show Jehovah's Witnesses the Greek word *nun* (meaning "now") in a Westcott and Hort New Testament (the basis of their *Kingdom Interlinear Translation of the Greek Scriptures,* 1969). The Watchtower translation committee translated "a god" in John 1:1 to get rid of the deity of Christ. They inserted the word "other" four times in Col. 1:16-17 to make Jesus a creature.

The Greek word translated "deity" in Col. 2:9 is *theotes.* Its meaning is "the state of being God, Godhead" (Thayer, *Greek-English Lexicon,* p. 288). The *New World Translation of the Holy Scriptures* (1970) of the Watchtower incorrectly translates Col. 2:9, "It is in him that all the fulness of the divine quality dwells bodily." The Spirit-inspired apostle, however, states that not merely God's quality but God's very nature, God Himself, dwells in Jesus.

In Rev. 3:14 Jesus Christ is called "the Beginning of God's creation." Jehovah's Witnesses interpret this term to mean that He is the first creation of Jehovah. The Greek word for "beginning" is *arche.* The *Greek-English Lexicon* of Thayer (p. 77) indicates that in Rev. 3:14 *arche* means "the origin, active cause." Jesus Christ is not the first creation of God, but the origin or originator of all creation. He is the Creator, not a creature.

The Kingdom Interlinear Translation of the Greek Scriptures (1969) renders John 8:58: "Jesus said to them: Most truly I say to you, Before Abraham came into existence, I have been." It has a footnote to the effect that "I have been" is properly rendered in the perfect tense after the aorist infinitive clause "Before Abraham came into existence." The truth is that Jesus speaks of Himself in the present tense: *eimi* in the Greek. The correct way to translate this Greek word is "I am." Jesus is making a sharp contrast between Abraham and Himself. Abraham came into existence at a certain point of time. Unlike Abraham, Jesus is independent of any beginning of time. He exists and has always existed.

The New World Translation of the Christian Greek Scriptures (1950), p. 312) has a footnote concerning John 8:58 that states "I have been" is the perfect indefinite tense. The fact is that there is no such tense in the Greek language, in which the New Testament was first written.

Key Questions to Ask Jehovah's Witnesses

If Jehovah's Witnesses insist on talking, ask questions and seek clarification. This puts them on the defensive, where they have been taught to keep you. The following questions have been asked many times with success.

1. Jehovah's Witnesses say that Jesus rose from the dead. Yet they do not believe that His body, soul, or spirit rose. They just say "He rose." Ask: Who is the "He" who rose? (See dialogue: The Resurrection of Jesus Christ Versus His Re-creation)

2. Do Jehovah's Witnesses worship Jeus? Some say they do. Others

say they don't. Their *New World Translation* says He is to be worshiped by angels as commanded by Jehovah (Heb. 1:6). Their books say creatures are not to be worshiped. Their charter says that their Kingdom Halls are built for the "public Christian worship of Almighty God and Jesus Christ." (See Chapter: Is It Right to Worship Jesus?)

3. Jehovah's Witnesses believe that in the beginning Jesus was created as the archangel Michael in heaven. Then, they say, He went out of existence and was born on earth as a man. Jesus then became "dead and dead forever." Three days after Jesus' death Jehovah created a spirit creature, Michael. Since Jehovah's Witnesses do not believe that God took on the nature of a man in Jesus, they believe in three separate creations of Jesus Christ. We ask: How can you say these three individuals are the same person, if there is no continuity between them? Michael, the archangel, did not have the authority to rebuke Satan (Jude 9). But Jesus rebuked Satan in the wilderness (Matt. 4:10). How then, we ask, can you say Jesus is Michael?

4. Jesus is called the "First and Last" in Rev. 1:17. Jehovah is spoken of as "First and Last" (the eternal One) in Is. 44:6. How can there be two firsts and two lasts?

5. If Jehovah always and only dwells in the highest heavens, how could He be "in Christ"? (2 Cor. 5:19).

6. Jehovah's Witnesses say God is not omnipresent. How then can He fill heaven and earth? (Jer. 23:24).

7. How could the Father be greater than Jesus (John 14:28) but equal with Jesus according to John 5:18? Note: Because Jesus is the God-man, there are many paradoxes of this kind. These seeming contradictions present no problem to us but they do to Jehovah's Witnesses, who think Jesus is only a man. For example, Jehovah's Witnesses ask: "Who ran the universe during the three days that Jesus was dead? If Jesus was God, then during Jesus' death God was dead and in the grave." The answer is that Jesus' divine nature was always associated with His human nature, for "In Him the whole fulness of deity dwells bodily" (Col. 2:9). For that reason His sacrifice on the cross was a sufficient ransom for all mankind.

8. In connection with the dual nature of Christ, ask such questions as: How could Jesus be both the Shepherd (John 10:14) and the Lamb (John 1:29)? How could He be born in Bethlehem (Micah 5:2) and yet be everlasting (Is. 9:6)?

9. On a number of occasions (for example, John 4:34, John 20:21, etc.) Jesus stated that the Father sent Him. Jehovah's Witnesses claim this proves that God, the Sender, is greater than Jesus, the sent One *(Things in Which It Is Impossible for God to Lie,* 1965, p. 269). Yet in Is. 48:16 it is written: "The Lord God has sent Me and His Spirit." "Me" refers to the Creator whose hand laid the foundation of the earth (Is. 48:12-13). Can the Creator be less than the One who sent Him?

10. If death is the termination of existence, as the Watchtower insists, what did Paul mean when he spoke of being "away from the body" and "at home with the Lord"? (2 Cor. 5:8).

11. If the Holy Spirit is a force and not a living person, how can He love?—be grieved?—speak?

12. How can the Lord of hosts send the Lord of hosts? (Zech. 2:8-11).

13. When Jehovah's Witnesses mention the kingdom, ask them if it is true that the kingdom is heavenly. Then ask why they pray in the Lord's Prayer, "Thy kingdom come, Thy will be done on earth"?

14. Jehovah's Witnesses baptize in the name of the Father, the Son (a creature according to Jehovah's Witnesses), and the spirit-directed organization (*The Watchtower*, 6-1-85, p. 30). What right do they have to change the words of Jesus in Matthew 28:19?

15. The Bible speaks of God as one Lord in Deut. 6:4. Why does the Bible not talk of Moses as being one Moses or Paul as being one Paul? The answer is that God is triune. (See reference to the one, united Lord, Deut. 6:4 in the chapter entitled "One God—Three Divine Personalities.")

16. Jehovah's Witnesses say that we teach three Gods because 1 + 1 + 1 = 3. But the word for "fulness" of deity in Col. 2:9 means volume. How do you get volume? By multiplying—1 x 1 x 1 = 1.

17. God made Himself known to the Jews by the personal name Jehovah or Yahweh. The exact English form of this word is uncertain since the Hebrew word is made up of four consonants YHWH without vowel sounds. The ancient Jews regarded this name as so sacred that whenever they came to the word "Jehovah" in the Scriptures, they spoke the word *Adonai* (Lord) instead. The Revised Standard Version following the Jewish practice renders YHWH "the LORD" (in capital letters) for two reasons: "(1) The word 'Jehovah' does not accurately represent any form of the Name ever used in Hebrew; and (2) the use of any proper name for the one and only God, as though there were other gods from whom He had to be distinguished, was discontinued in Judaism before the Christian era and is entirely inappropriate for the universal faith of the Christian church." The King James Version also uses the translation LORD with exceptions like Ex. 6:3 and Ps. 83:18, where it translates "Jehovah."

Jehovah's Witnesses insist that the divine name "Jehovah" must be used. It is not sufficient, they say, to call Him God *(Make Sure of All Things,* 1965, p. 264). The New World Bible translators, by using passages and expressions from the Hebrew Scriptures, have restored the name Jehovah throughout the New Testament with some notable exceptions. One of these exceptions is Phil. 2:10-11, which is based on Is. 45:22-23. Why weren't the New World Bible translators consistent and properly translate Phil. 2:11 "and every tongue confess that Jesus Christ is Jehovah, to the glory of God the Father"?

Another example of their inconsistency is 1 Peter 3:15. It is a quotation of Is. 8:13, which reads, "The LORD [Jehovah] of hosts . . . let Him be your fear, and let Him be your dread." Why did not the New World Bible Translation Committee follow their own rule and translate 1 Peter 3:15 "In your hearts reverence Christ as Jehovah"?

A Final Word

May this book be a permanent blessing to you and may you in turn use it to be a blessing to others to the glory of God—Father, Son, and Holy Spirit.

Bibliography

Dencher, Ted, *Why I Left Jehovah's Witnesses*. Fort Washington, Pa. 19034: Christian Literature Crusade, 1966.

Gruss, Edmond C., *We Left Jehovah's Witnesses*. Grand Rapids, Mich.: Baker Book House, 1974.

Hoekema, Anthony A., *The Four Major Cults*. Grand Rapids, Mich.: Eerdmans, 1963.

Martin, Walter R., *The Kingdom of the Cults*. Minneapolis, Minn.: Bethany Fellowship, Inc., 1965.

Martin, Walter R. and Norman H. Klann, *Jehovah of the Watchtower*. Chicago: Moody Press, 1974.

Metzger, Bruce M., *The Jehovah's Witnesses and Jesus Christ*. Princeton, N. J.: Theological Book Agency, Theology Today, April 1953 Reprint.

Van Buskirk, Michael, *The Scholastic Dishonesty of the Watchtower*. Santa Ana, Calif. 92702: (P. O. Box 1783) May 1975.

Watch Tower Bible & Tract Society Publications Quoted

The New World Translation of the Christian Greek Scriptures, 1950
Let God Be True, Revised 1952
Make Sure of All Things, Copyright 1953 and Copyright 1965
You May Survive Armageddon into God's New World, 1955
From Paradise Lost to Paradise Regained, 1958
Things in Which It Is Impossible for God to Lie, 1965
The Truth That Leads to Eternal Life, 1968
The Kingdom Interlinear Translation of the Greek Scriptures, 1969
New World Translation of the Holy Scriptures, Revised 1970
Aid to Bible Understanding, 1971
Is This Life All There Is? 1974
1977 Yearbook of Jehovah's Witnesses, 1976